D1042376

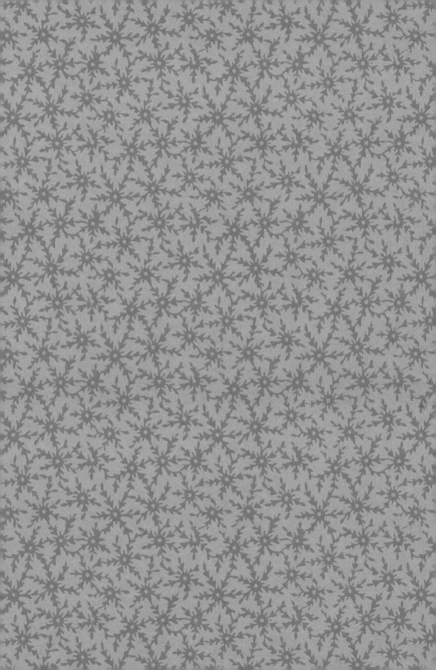

To:

Grammie

From:

Jacob, Riley & Adam

Date:

Mar. 26, 2013

Happy 80th
Birthday !
We love you !
XOXO

© 2011 Summerside Press™
Minneapolis 55438
www.summersidepress.com

Amazing Grace
A *Pocket Inspirations* Book

ISBN 978-1-60936-272-0

Scripture references are from the following sources: The Holy Bible, New
International Version®, NIV®. Copyright © 1973, 1978, 1984 by Biblica, Inc.™
Used by permission of Zondervan. All rights reserved worldwide. The New
King James Version (NKJV). Copyright © 1982 by Thomas Nelson, Inc. Used by
permission. The New American Standard Bible® (NASB). Copyright © 1960, 1962,
1963, 1968, 1971, 1972, 1973, 1975, 1977, 1995 by The Lockman Foundation.
Used by permission. The Holy Bible, New Living Translation® (NLT). Copyright
© 1996, 2004. Used by permission of Tyndale House Publishers, Inc., Wheaton,
Illinois 60189. *The Message* (MSG) © 1993, 1994, 1995, 1996, 2000, 2001, 2002 by
Eugene Peterson. Used by permission of NavPress, Colorado Springs, CO. The New
Century Version® (NCV). Copyright © 1987, 1988, 1991 by Thomas Nelson, Inc.
Used by permission. All rights reserved.

†Amazing Grace words by John Newton, Olney Hymns (London: W. Oliver, 1779).
Public Domain. The seventh stanza on the final page of the journal is of unknown
origin. It was originally noted as the last stanza of *Jerusalem, My Happy Home*.

Excluding Scripture verses and divine pronouns, in some quotations references to
men and masculine pronouns have been replaced with gender-neutral or feminine
references. Additionally, in some quotations we have carefully updated verb forms
and wordings that may distract modern readers.

Compiled by Barbara Farmer
Designed by Lisa & Jeff Franke

*Summerside Press™ is an inspirational publisher offering fresh, irresistible books to uplift
the heart and engage the mind.*

Printed in China.

Amazing Grace

A *Pocket Inspirations* Book

Pi Pocket
INSPIRATIONS

summerside
PRESS

Contents

*Amazing grace! How sweet the sound
That saved a wretch like me!
I once was lost, but now am found;
Was blind, but now I see.*

So Amazing

Not that we deserve it, not that we can earn it,
but that we know how precious and valuable a gift it is.
That's what makes grace so amazing!

Grace comes free of charge to people who
do not deserve it and I am one of those people....
Now I am trying in my own small way to
pipe the tune of grace. I do so because I know,
more surely than I know anything,
that any pang of healing or forgiveness or
goodness I have ever felt comes solely
from the grace of God.

Philip Yancey

May the grace of the Lord Jesus Christ,
and the love of God, and the fellowship
of the Holy Spirit be with you all.

2 Corinthians 13:14 niv

The most glorious promises of God are
generally fulfilled in such a wondrous manner
that He steps forth to save us at a time when
there is the least appearance of it.

KARL HEINRICH VON BOGATZKY

Grace is...a boundless offering of
God's self to us, suffering with us,
overflowing with tenderness.
Grace is God's passion.

GERALD G. MAY

*Receive and experience
the amazing grace of...Christ,
deep, deep within yourselves.*

PHILIPPIANS 4:23 MSG

Infinite Love

An infinite God can give all of Himself
to each of His children. He does not distribute
Himself that each may have a part,
but to each one He gives all of Himself
as fully as if there were no others....
His love has not changed.
It hasn't cooled off, and it needs no increase
because He has already loved us
with infinite love and there is no way
that infinitude can be increased....
He is the same yesterday, today, and forever!

A. W. TOZER

Our ever growing soul and its capacities
can be satisfied only in the infinite God.

SADHU SUNDAR SINGH

Infinite and yet personal, personal and yet infinite,
God may be trusted because He is the True One.
He is true, He acts truly, and He speaks truly....
God's truthfulness is therefore foundational
for His trustworthiness.

OS GUINNESS

At the very heart and foundation of all God's dealings
with us, however dark and mysterious they may be,
we must dare to believe in and assert the infinite,
unmerited, and unchanging love of God.

L. B. COWMAN

*That you, being rooted and grounded in love,
may be able to know the love of Christ
which surpasses knowledge.*

EPHESIANS 3:17–18 NASB

God's Favor

God longs to give favor—that is,
spiritual strength and health—to those
who seek Him, and Him alone.
He grants spiritual favors and victories,
not because the one who seeks Him
is holier than anyone else,
but in order to make His holy beauty
and His great redeeming power known....
For it is through the living witness
of others that we are drawn to God at all.
It is because of His creatures, and His work
in them, that we come to praise Him.

TERESA OF AVILA

It is not what we do that matters, *but what a
sovereign God chooses to do through us.*
God doesn't want our success; He wants us.

CHARLES COLSON

Each one of us is God's special work of art.
Through us, He teaches and inspires, delights
and encourages, informs and uplifts all those
who view our lives. God, the master artist,
is most concerned about expressing Himself—
His thoughts and His intentions—through what
He paints in our character.... [He] wants to
paint a beautiful portrait of His Son
in and through your life.
A painting like no other in all of time.

JONI EARECKSON TADA

*God had special plans for me
and set me apart for his work....
He called me through his grace.*

GALATIANS 1:15 NCV

Gifts of Grace

Grace is something you can never get but can
only be given. There's no way to earn it or deserve it
or bring it about anymore than you can deserve the
taste of raspberries and cream or earn good looks....
A good night's sleep is grace and so are good dreams.
Most tears are grace. The smell of rain is grace.
Somebody loving you is grace.

FREDERICK BUECHNER

The secret of life is that all we have and are
is a gift of grace to be shared.

LLOYD JOHN OGILVIE

All those who live with any degree of serenity
live by some assurance of grace.

REINHOLD NIEBUHR

Walk in a manner worthy of the calling with which
you have been called...being diligent to preserve
the unity of the Spirit in the bond of peace....
To each one of us grace was given
according to the measure of Christ's gift.

EPHESIANS 4:2–3, 7 NASB

The beauty of grace—our only permanent deliverance
from guilt—is that it meets us where we are
and gives us what we don't deserve.

CHARLES R. SWINDOLL

*God loved us, and through his grace
he gave us a good hope and encouragement.*

2 THESSALONIANS 2:16 NCV

All Is Well

It's usually through our hard times,
the unexpected and not-according-to-plan times,
that we experience God in more intimate ways.
We discover an unquenchable longing
to know Him more. It's a passion that isn't
concerned that life fall within certain
predictable lines, but a passion that pursues
God and knows He is relentless in
His pursuit of each one of us.

WENDY MOORE

Lord, you have been our dwelling place
throughout all generations.
Before the mountains were born
or you brought forth the earth and the world,
from everlasting to everlasting you are God.

PSALM 90:1-2 NIV

In difficulties, I can drink freely of
God's power and experience His touch of
refreshment and blessing—much like
an invigorating early spring rain.

ANABEL GILLHAM

A living, loving God can and does make
His presence felt, can and does speak to us
in the silence of our hearts, can and does
warm and caress us till we no longer doubt
that He is near, that He is here.

BRENNAN MANNING

Before me, even as behind,
God is, and all is well.

JOHN GREENLEAF WHITTIER

*Give all your worries and cares to God,
for he cares about you.*

1 PETER 5:7 NLT

Grace and Gratitude

Grace and gratitude belong together
like heaven and earth. Grace evokes gratitude
like the voice an echo. Gratitude follows
grace as thunder follows lightning.

KARL BARTH

Life itself, every bit of health that we enjoy,
every hour of liberty and free enjoyment,
the ability to see, to hear, to speak, to think,
and to imagine—all this comes from
the hand of God. We show our gratitude
by giving back to Him a part of that
which He has given to us.

BILLY GRAHAM

May you be filled with joy, always thanking
the Father. He has enabled you to share in
the inheritance that belongs to his people,
who live in the light.

COLOSSIANS 1:11–12 NLT

Gratitude consists in a watchful, minute attention
to the particulars of our state, and to the multitude of
God's gifts, taken one by one. It fills us with a
consciousness that God loves and cares for us,
even to the least event and smallest need of life.

HENRY EDWARD MANNING

I will bless the LORD at all times;
His praise shall continually be in my mouth.

PSALM 34:1 NASB

God of Grace

Look deep within yourself and recognize
what brings life and grace into your heart.
It is this that can be shared with those
around you. You are loved by God.
This is an inspiration to love.

CHRISTOPHER DE VINCK

The Lord's chief desire is to reveal Himself to you
and, in order for Him to do that, He gives you
abundant grace. The Lord gives you the
experience of enjoying His presence.
He touches you, and His touch is so delightful
that, more than ever, you are drawn
inwardly to Him.

MADAME JEANNE GUYON

It is my calling to treat every human being with
grace and dignity, to treat every person, whether
encountered in a palace or a gas station,
as a life made in the image of God.

SHEILA WALSH

To be grateful is to recognize the love of God
in everything He has given us—and He has given us
everything. Every breath we draw is a gift of His love,
every moment of existence is a gift of grace,
for it brings with it immense graces from Him.

THOMAS MERTON

*Set your hope fully on the
grace to be given you when
Jesus Christ is revealed.*

1 PETER 1:13 NIV

Open Hearts

The "air" which our souls need also envelops
all of us at all times and on all sides.
God is round about us in Christ on every hand,
with many-sided and all-sufficient grace.
All we need to do is to open our hearts.

OLE HALLESBY

God wants you to know Him as personally
as He knows you. He craves a genuine
relationship with you....
He didn't make us robots, pre-programmed
to love Him and follow Him. He gave us free
will and leaves it to us to choose to spend
time with Him. That way it's genuine.
That way it's a real relationship.

TOM RICHARDS

What was invisible we behold,
What was unknown is known.
Open our eyes to the light of grace,
Unloose our hearts from fear,
Be with us in the strength of love,
Lead us in the hope of courage.

EVELYN FRANCIS CAPEL

Lord, give me an open heart to find You everywhere,
to glimpse the heaven enfolded in a bud,
and to experience eternity in the smallest act of love.

MOTHER TERESA

*God not only loves you very much
but also has put his hand on you
for something special.*

1 THESSALONIANS 1:4 MSG

Rich Grace

The LORD gives righteousness and justice
to all who are treated unfairly:...
He will not constantly accuse us,
nor remain angry forever.
He does not punish us for all our sins;
he does not deal harshly with us, as we deserve.
For his unfailing love toward those
who fear him is as great as the height of
the heavens above the earth.
He has removed our sins as far from us
as the east is from the west.

PSALM 103:6, 9–12 NLT

By Jesus' gracious, kindly Spirit, He moves
in our lives sharing His very own life with us....
He introduces the exotic fruits of His own
person into the prepared soil of our hearts,
there they take root and flourish.

W. PHILIP KELLER

From the fullness of his grace we have all
received one blessing after another.

JOHN 1:16 NIV

Lord...give me only Your love and
Your grace. With this I am rich enough,
and I have no more to ask.

IGNATIUS OF LOYOLA

His overflowing love
delights to make us partakers of
the bounties He graciously imparts.

HANNAH MORE

*O LORD, be gracious to us; we long for you.
Be our strength every morning.*

ISAIAH 33:2 NIV

His Perfection

We don't have to be perfect.... We are asked
only to be real, trusting in His perfection
to cover our imperfection,
knowing that one day we will finally be all that
Christ saved us for and wants us to be.

GIGI GRAHAM TCHIVIDJIAN

When perfection comes, the imperfect disappears....
Now we see but a poor reflection as in a mirror;
then we shall see face to face. Now I know in part;
then I shall know fully, even as I am fully known.

1 CORINTHIANS 13:10, 12 NIV

There is no one so far lost that Jesus cannot
find him and cannot save him.

ANDREW MURRAY

God is looking for people who will come
in simple dependence upon His grace,
and rest in simple faith upon His greatness.
At this very moment, He's looking at you.

JACK HAYFORD

I am not what I ought to be,
I am not what I wish to be,
I am not what I hope to be;
but, by the grace of God,
I am not what I was.

JOHN NEWTON

*For You have worked wonders,
plans formed long ago,
with perfect faithfulness.*

ISAIAH 25:1 NASB

God Is Good

All we are and all we have is by the...love of God!
The goodness of God is infinitely more wonderful
than we will ever be able to comprehend.

A. W. TOZER

Open your mouth and taste, open your
eyes and see—how good GOD is.
Blessed are you who run to him.
Worship GOD if you want the best;
worship opens doors to all his goodness.

PSALM 34:8–9 MSG

The Lord's goodness surrounds us at every moment.
I walk through it almost with difficulty,
as through thick grass and flowers.

R. W. BARBER

All that is good, all that is true,
all that is beautiful...be it great or small,
be it perfect or fragmentary,
natural as well as supernatural,
moral as well as material,
comes from God.

JOHN HENRY NEWMAN

We walk without fear, full of hope and courage
and strength to do His will, waiting for the
endless good which He is always giving as
fast as He can get us able to take it in.

GEORGE MACDONALD

*I am still confident in this:
I will see the goodness of the LORD
in the land of the living.*

PSALM 27:13 NIV

'Twas grace that taught my heart to fear,
And grace my fears relieved;
How precious did that grace appear,
The hour I first believed!

My Fears Relieved

We sometimes fear to bring our troubles to God,
because they must seem so small to Him who
sits on the circle of the earth. But if they are
large enough to...endanger our welfare,
they are large enough to touch His heart of love.

R. A. TORREY

Grasp the fact that God is for you—
let this certainty make its impact on you
in relation to what you are up against
at this very moment; and you will find
in thus knowing God as your
sovereign protector, irrevocably committed
to you in the covenant of grace,
both freedom from fear
and new strength for the fight.

J. I. PACKER

You can be sure that God will take care of
everything you need, his generosity exceeding
even yours in the glory that pours from Jesus.
Our God and Father abounds in glory that
just pours out into eternity.

PHILIPPIANS 4:18–19 MSG

Every action of our lives touches
a chord that vibrates in Eternity.

EDWIN HUBBEL CHAPIN

*Cast your burden on the LORD,
And He shall sustain you.*

PSALM 55:22 NKJV

Blessing on Blessing

God is a rich and bountiful Father, and He does not
forget His children, nor withhold from them anything
which it would be to their advantage to receive.

J. K. MACLEAN

Strength, rest, guidance, grace, help,
sympathy, love—all from God to us!
What a list of blessings!

EVELYN STENBOCK

You're blessed when you're content with
just who you are—no more, no less.
That's the moment you find yourselves
proud owners of everything that can't be bought.

MATTHEW 5:5 MSG

If anyone would tell you the shortest,
surest way to happiness and all perfection,
he must tell you to make it a rule to yourself
to thank and praise God for everything
that happens to you. For it is certain that
whatever...happens to you, if you thank and
praise God for it, you turn it into a blessing.

WILLIAM LAW

God, who is love—who is, if I may
say it this way, made out of love—
simply cannot help but shed
blessing on blessing upon us.

HANNAH WHITALL SMITH

*I will send down showers in season;
there will be showers of blessing.*

EZEKIEL 34:26 NIV

Grace Abounds

To pray is to change. This is a great grace.
How good of God to provide a path whereby
our lives can be taken over by love and joy and
peace and patience and kindness and goodness
and faithfulness and gentleness and self-control.

RICHARD J. FOSTER

A life transformed by the power of God
is always a marvel and a miracle.

GERALDINE NICHOLAS

For God is, indeed, a wonderful Father who longs to
pour out His mercy upon us, and whose majesty
is so great that He can transform us from deep within.

TERESA OF AVILA

The wonder of our Lord is that He is so
accessible to us in the common things of our lives:
the cup of water...breaking of the bread...welcoming
children into our arms...fellowship over a meal...
giving thanks. A simple attitude of caring,
listening, and lovingly telling the truth.

NANCIE CARMICHAEL

If God is here for us and not elsewhere, then in fact
this place is holy and this moment is sacred.

ISABEL ANDERS

*God is able to make all grace abound to you,
so that in all things at all times...
you will abound in every good work.*

2 CORINTHIANS 9:8 NIV

Blessed Assurance

Peace of conscience, liberty of heart,
the sweetness of abandoning ourselves in the
hands of God, the joy of always seeing the light
grow in our hearts, finally, freedom from the fears
and insatiable desires of the times, multiply
a hundredfold the happiness which the true
children of God possess in the midst of
their [trials], if they are faithful.

FRANÇOIS FÉNELON

God Incarnate is the end of fear;
and the heart that realizes that He is
in the midst, that takes heed to
the assurance of His loving presence,
will be quiet in the midst of alarm.

F. B. MEYER

Come, Thou long-expected Jesus,
born to set Thy people free;
From our fears and sins release us;
let us find our rest in Thee.

CHARLES WESLEY

Today I give it all to Jesus:
my precious children, my mate, my hopes,
my plans and dreams and schemes,
my fears and failures—all.
Peace and contentment come
when the struggle ceases.

GLORIA GAITHER

*In peace I will lie down and sleep,
for you alone, O LORD,
will keep me safe.*

PSALM 4:8 NLT

Our Father

Incredible as it may seem, God wants our
companionship. He wants to have us close to Him.
He wants to be a father to us, to shield us,
to protect us, to counsel us, and to guide us
in our way through life.

BILLY GRAHAM

Don't we all long for a father...
who cares for us in spite of our failures?
We do have that type of a father.
A father who is at His best
when we are at our worst...
whose grace is strongest
when our devotion is weakest.

MAX LUCADO

This is your Father you are dealing with,
and he knows better than you what you need.
With a God like this loving you,
you can pray very simply.

MATTHEW 6:7 MSG

Christ knew His Father and offered Himself
unreservedly into His hands. If we let ourselves
be lost for His sake, trusting the same God as
Lord of all, we shall find safety where Christ
found His, in the arms of the Father.

ELISABETH ELLIOT

*Because we are his children, God has sent
the Spirit...into our hearts, prompting us
to call out, "Abba, Father."*

GALATIANS 4:6 NLT

Countless Beauties

Be still, and in the quiet moments,
listen to the voice of your heavenly Father.
His words can renew your spirit...
no one knows you and your needs like He does.

JANET L. WEAVER SMITH

Our Creator would never have made such
lovely days, and given us the deep hearts to
enjoy them, above and beyond all thought,
unless we were meant to be immortal.

NATHANIEL HAWTHORNE

All the world is an utterance of the Almighty.
Its countless beauties, its exquisite adaptations,
all speak to you of Him.

PHILLIPS BROOKS

The joyful birds prolong the strain,
their song with every spring renewed;
the air we breathe, and falling rain,
each softly whispers: God is good.

JOHN HAMPDEN GURNEY

Lord...give me the gift of faith to be
renewed and shared with others each day.
Teach me to live this moment only,
looking neither to the past with regret,
nor the future with apprehension.
Let love be my aim and my life a prayer.

ROSEANN ALEXANDER-ISHAM

*Worship the LORD in
the beauty of holiness!*

PSALM 96:9 NKJV

Trust Always

There is an activity of the spirit, silent, unseen,
which must be the dynamic of any form of
truly creative, fruitful trust. When we commit
a predicament, a possibility, a person to God
in genuine confidence, we do not merely step aside
and tap our foot until God comes through.
We remain involved. We remain in contact
with God in gratitude and praise.

EUGENIA PRICE

I trust You always though I may seem
to be lost and in the shadow of death.
I will not fear, for You are ever with me.
And You will never leave me
to face my perils alone.

THOMAS MERTON

Yea, though I walk through the valley
of the shadow of death, I will fear no evil;
for You are with me; Your rod and
Your staff, they comfort me.

PSALM 23:4 NKJV

Trust in your Redeemer's strength...
exercise what faith you have, and by and by
He shall rise upon you with healing
beneath His wings. Go from faith to faith
and you shall receive blessing upon blessing.

CHARLES H. SPURGEON

*Trust in the LORD with all your heart;
and lean not on your own understanding.*

PROVERBS 3:5 NKJV

Encountering God

We encounter God in the ordinariness of life,
not in the search for spiritual highs and
extraordinary, mystical experiences, but in
our simple presence in life.

BRENNAN MANNING

God is with us in the midst of our daily, routine lives. In the
middle of cleaning the house
or driving somewhere in the pickup....
Often it's in the middle of the most mundane task
that He lets us know He is there with us.
We realize, then, that there can be no
"ordinary" moments for people who
live their lives with Jesus.

MICHAEL CARD

It is through man's encounter with God
that he reaches his highest destiny.

CAROL GISH

Much of what is sacred is hidden in the
ordinary, everyday moments of our lives.
To see something of the sacred
in those moments takes slowing down
so we can live our lives more reflectively.

KEN GIRE

If each moment is sacred—a time and place
where we encounter God—life itself is sacred.

JEAN M. BLOMQUIST

*This is how we experience his
deep and abiding presence in us:
by the Spirit he gave us.*

1 JOHN 3:24 MSG

Dare to Believe

Regardless of whether we feel strong or weak
in our faith, we remember that our assurance
is not based upon our ability to conjure up
some special feeling. Rather, it is built upon a
confident assurance in the faithfulness of God.
We focus on His trustworthiness and
especially on His steadfast love.

RICHARD J. FOSTER

So faith bounds forward to its goal in God,
and love can trust her Lord to lead her there;
upheld by Him my soul is following hard,
till God has fully fulfilled my deepest prayer.

FREDERICK BROOK

Faith is not belief without proof,
but trust without reservations.

ELTON TRUEBLOOD

The grace is God's: the faith is ours.
God gave us the free will with which to choose.
God gave us the capacity to believe and trust.

BILLY GRAHAM

At the very heart and foundation of all God's
dealings with us,...we must dare to believe
in and assert the infinite, unmerited,
and unchanging love of God.

L. B. COWMAN

*I trust in your unfailing love.
I will rejoice because you
have rescued me.*

PSALM 13:5 NLT

God of Promise

For as the rain comes down,
and the snow from heaven,
and do not return there,
but water the earth,
and make it bring forth and bud,
that it may give seed to the sower
and bread to the eater, so shall
My word be that goes forth from My mouth;
it shall not return to Me void,
but it shall accomplish what I please,
and it shall prosper in the thing
for which I sent it.

ISAIAH 55:10–11 NKJV

God writes with a pen that never blots,
speaks with a tongue that never slips,
and acts with a hand that never fails.

HUBERT VAN ZELLER

Be assured, if you walk with Him and
look to Him and expect help from Him,
He will never fail you.

GEORGE MUELLER

The light of God surrounds me;
The love of God enfolds me;
The power of God protects me;
The presence of God watches over me.
Wherever I am, God is.

God is the God of promise. He keeps His word,
even when that seems impossible.

COLIN URQUHART

*The LORD always keeps his promises;
he is gracious in all he does.*

PSALM 145:13 NLT

I Believe

I believe in God, the Father Almighty,
maker of heaven and earth.

And in Jesus Christ, His only Son, our Lord,
who was conceived by the Holy Spirit,
and born of the virgin Mary,
suffered under Pontius Pilate,
was crucified, dead, and buried.
He descended into hell.
The third day He rose again from the dead.
He ascended into heaven
and sitteth at the right hand of
God the Father Almighty.
From thence He will come to judge
the quick and the dead.

I believe in the Holy Spirit,
the Holy Christian Church,
the communion of saints,
the forgiveness of sins,
the resurrection of the body,
and the life everlasting. Amen.

THE APOSTLES' CREED

To believe in God starts
with a conclusion about Him,
develops into confidence in Him, and
then matures into a conversation with Him.

STUART BRISCOE

The goal of grace is to create a love relationship
between God and us who believe, the kind
of relationship for which we were first made.
And the bond of fellowship by which God
binds Himself to us is His covenant.

J. I. PACKER

*You have this faith and love because
of your hope, and what you hope for
is kept safe for you in heaven.*

COLOSSIANS 1:5 NCV

Through many dangers, toils and snares,
I have already come;
'Tis grace has brought me safe thus far,
And grace will lead me home.

God's Nearness

Do you believe that God is near?
He wants you to. He wants you to know
that He is in the midst of your world.
Wherever you are as you read these words,
He is present. In your car. On the plane.
In your office, your bedroom, your den. He's near.
And He is more than near. He is active.

MAX LUCADO

I have sought Thy nearness;
With all my heart have I called Thee,
And going out to meet Thee
I found Thee coming toward me.

YEHUDA HALEVI

Have confidence in God's mercy, for when
you think He is a long way from you,
He is often quite near.

THOMAS À KEMPIS

God still draws near to us in the ordinary,
commonplace, everyday experiences and places....
He comes in surprising ways.

HENRY GARIEPY

It is God to whom and with whom we travel,
and while He is the End of our journey,
He is also at every stopping place.

ELISABETH ELLIOT

*Draw near to God and
He will draw near to you.*

JAMES 4:8 NASB

Redeemed

Praise the LORD, O my soul,
and forget not all his benefits—
who forgives all your sins
and heals all your diseases,
who redeems your life from the pit
and crowns you with love and compassion,
who satisfies your desires with good things
so that your youth is renewed like the eagle's.

PSALM 103:2–5 NIV

When we focus on God, the scene changes.
He's in control of our lives; nothing lies
outside the realm of His redemptive grace.
Even when we make mistakes,
fail in relationships, or deliberately make
bad choices, God can redeem us.

PENELOPE J. STOKES

I think of my blessed Redeemer,
I think of Him all the day long:
I sing, for I cannot be silent;
His love is the theme of my song.

FANNY CROSBY

Jesus is the Savior,
but He is even more than that!
He is more than a Forgiver of our sins.
He is even more than our Provider
of eternal life. He is our Redeemer!
He is the One who is ready to recover
and restore what the power of sin
and death has taken from us.

JACK HAYFORD

*But the LORD will redeem those
who serve him. No one who takes refuge
in him will be condemned.*

PSALM 34:22 NLT

He Leads Me

Living a life of faith means never knowing
where you are being led. But it does mean
loving and knowing the One who is leading.
It is literally a life of faith...a life of knowing
Him who calls us to go.

OSWALD CHAMBERS

A new path lies before us;
We're not sure where it leads;
But God goes on before us,
Providing all our needs.
This path, so new, so different
Exciting as we climb,
Will guide us in His perfect will
Until the end of time.

LINDA MAURICE

God guides us, despite our uncertainties and our
vagueness, even through our failings and mistakes....
He leads us step by step, from event to event.
Only afterwards, as we look back over the way we
have come and reconsider certain important moments
in our lives in the light of all that has followed them,
or when we survey the whole progress of our lives,
do we experience the feeling of having been led
without knowing it, the feeling that God
has mysteriously guided us.

PAUL TOURNIER

*Lead me by your truth and teach me,
for you are the God who saves me.
All day long I put my hope in you.*

PSALM 25:5 NLT

Shining Promises

Our feelings do not affect God's facts.
They may blow up, like clouds, and cover the
eternal things that we do most truly believe.
We may not see the shining of the promises—
but they still shine! [His strength] is not for
one moment less because of our human weakness.

Amy Carmichael

We do not know how this is true—
where would faith be if we did?—
but we do know that all things that
happen are full of shining seed.
Light is sown for us—not darkness.

But He knows the way I take;
when He has tried me,
I shall come forth as gold.

Job 23:10 nasb

God's promises are like the stars;
the darker the night the brighter they shine.

DAVID NICHOLAS

God has not promised skies always blue,
flower-strewn pathways all our lives through;
God has not promised sun without rain,
joy without sorrow, peace without pain.
But God has promised strength for the day,
rest for the labor, light for the way,
grace for the trials, help from above,
unfailing sympathy, undying love.

ANNIE JOHNSON FLINT

*Not one word has failed
of all His good promise.*

1 KINGS 8:56 NASB

Strong Refuge

We know that [God] gives us
every grace, every abundant grace;
and though we are so weak of ourselves,
this grace is able to carry us through
every obstacle and difficulty.

ELIZABETH ANN SETON

The LORD is good,
a strong refuge when trouble comes.
He is close to those who trust in him.

NAHUM 1:7 NLT

If the Lord be with us, we have no cause of fear.
His eye is upon us, His arm over us, His ear open
to our prayer—His grace sufficient,
His promise unchangeable.

JOHN NEWTON

Jesus Christ is no security against storms,
but He is perfect security in storms.
He has never promised you an easy passage,
only a safe landing.

L. B. Cowman

Do not take over much thought for tomorrow.
God, who has led you safely on so far,
will lead you on to the end. Be altogether at rest
in the loving holy confidence which you
ought to have in His heavenly Providence.

Francis de Sales

For You are my strong refuge.
My mouth is filled with Your praise
And with Your glory all day long.

Psalm 71:7 nasb

God Is for Us

Don't be afraid, I've redeemed you.
I've called your name. You're mine.
When you're in over your head,
I'll be there with you.
When you're in rough waters,
you will not go down.
When you're between a rock and a hard place,
it won't be a dead end—
Because I am GOD, your personal God,
The Holy of Israel, your Savior.
I paid a huge price for you...!
That's how much you mean to me!
That's how much I love you!

ISAIAH 43:1–4 MSG

God not only knows us, but He values us highly
in spite of all He knows.... You and I are the
creatures He prizes above the rest of His creation.

JOHN FISHER

Lord Jesus Christ, I thank You
For all the benefits You have won for me,
For all the pains and insults that
You have borne for me.
Most merciful redeemer,
friend and brother,
May I know You more clearly,
Love You more dearly
And follow You more nearly
Day by day. Amen.

RICHARD OF CHICHESTER

*If God is for us,
who can be against us?*

ROMANS 8:31 NKJV

Restoring Love

God's loving initiative to step into time and
space to restore us to Himself is still a cause
for wonder and praise.

GLORIA GAITHER

There is no rest in the heart of God
until He knows that we are at rest in His grace.

LLOYD JOHN OGILVIE

Keep a firm grip on the faith. The suffering
won't last forever. It won't be long before
this generous God who has great plans for us
in Christ—eternal and glorious plans they are!—
will have you put together and on your feet for good.

1 PETER 5:10–11 MSG

Guidance is a sovereign act. Not merely
does God will to guide us by showing us
His way...whatever mistakes we may make,
we shall come safely home.
Slippings and strayings there will be, no doubt,
but the everlasting arms are beneath us;
we shall be caught, rescued, restored.
This is God's promise; this is how good He is.
And our self-distrust, while keeping us humble,
must not cloud the joy with which we
lean on our faithful covenant God.

J. I. PACKER

*The LORD longs to be gracious to you;
he rises to show you compassion.*

ISAIAH 30:18 NIV

Every Need

God wants nothing from us except our needs,
and these furnish Him with room to display
His bounty when He supplies them freely....
Not what I have, but what I do not have,
is the first point of contact between
my soul and God.

CHARLES H. SPURGEON

Jesus Christ has brought every need, every joy,
every gratitude, every hope of ours before God.
He accompanies us and brings us
into the presence of God.

DIETRICH BONHOEFFER

You can trust God right now to supply all
your needs for today. And if your needs are
more tomorrow, His supply will be greater also.

Knowing God is putting your trust in Him.
Trust that He loves you and will provide
for your every need. When we know God,
we know Him like a personal friend....
God is for us! He will never leave us.

TOM RICHARDS

Each of us may be sure that if God sends us
on stony paths He will provide us with strong shoes,
and He will not send us out on any journey
for which He does not equip us well.

ALEXANDER MACLAREN

*You are my strength;
I wait for you to rescue me,
for you, O God, are my fortress.*

PSALM 59:9 NLT

It Is Well

When peace like a river attendeth my way,
when sorrow like sea-billows roll;
Whatever my lot, Thou hast taught me to say,
"It is well, it is well with my soul."

HORATIO G. SPAFFORD

I have told you these things, so that in me
you may have peace. In this world you
will have trouble. But take heart!
I have overcome the world.

JOHN 16:33 NIV

The peace of God is that eternal calm which
lies far too deep down to be reached
by any external trouble or disturbance.

ARTHUR. T. PIERSON

Only Christ Himself, who slept in the boat in the
storm and then spoke calm to the wind and waves,
can stand beside us when we are in a panic and
say to us Peace. It will not be explainable.
It transcends human understanding.
And there is nothing else like it
in the whole wide world.

ELISABETH ELLIOT

How calmly may we commit ourselves
to the hands of Him who bears up the world.

JEAN PAUL RICHTER

*The peace of God, which surpasses
all understanding, will guard your
hearts and minds through Christ Jesus.*

PHILIPPIANS 4:7 NKJV

Surpassing Grace

God, being rich in mercy, because of His
great love with which He loved us,
even when we were dead in our transgressions,
made us alive together with Christ
(by grace you have been saved), and raised us
up with Him, and seated us with Him in the
heavenly places in Christ Jesus, so that in the
ages to come He might show the surpassing riches
of His grace in kindness toward us in Christ Jesus.
For by grace you have been saved through faith;
and that not of yourselves, it is the gift of God;
not as a result of works, so that no one may boast.

EPHESIANS 2:4–9 NASB

God's grace is the oil that fills the lamp of love.

HENRY WARD BEECHER

Grace means that God already loves us as much
as an infinite God can possibly love.

PHILIP YANCEY

Grace is no stationary thing, it is ever becoming.
It is flowing straight out of God's heart.
Grace does nothing but re-form and convey God.
Grace makes the soul conformable to the will of God.
God, the ground of the soul, and grace go together.

MEISTER ECKHART

*The LORD is compassionate and gracious,
slow to anger, abounding in love.*

PSALM 103:8 NIV

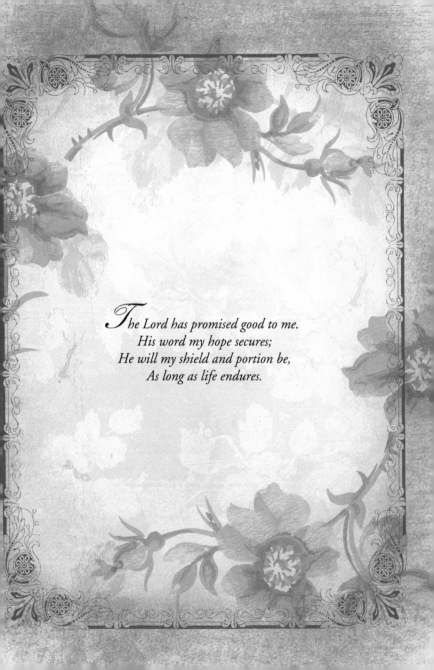

The Lord has promised good to me.
His word my hope secures;
He will my shield and portion be,
As long as life endures.

A New Day

Every day we live is a priceless gift of God,
loaded with possibilities to learn something new,
to gain fresh insights.

DALE EVANS ROGERS

God give me joy in the common things:
In the dawn that lures, the eve that sings.
In the new grass sparkling after rain,
In the late wind's wild and weird refrain;
In the springtime's spacious field of gold,
In the precious light by winter doled....
God give me joy in the tasks that press,
In the memories that burn and bless;
In the thought that life has love to spend,
In the faith that God's at journey's end.

THOMAS CURTIS CLARK

You wake up in the morning, and lo! your purse
is magically filled with twenty-four hours
of the magic tissue of the universe of your life.
No one can take it from you. No one receives
either more or less than you receive.
Waste your infinitely precious commodity
as much as you will, and the supply will never be
withheld from you. Moreover, you cannot
draw on the future. Impossible to get into debt.
You can only waste the passing movements.
You cannot waste tomorrow. It is kept for you.

ARNOLD BENNETT

His compassions never fail.
They are new every morning;
great is your faithfulness.

LAMENTATIONS 3:22–23 NIV

Grace Is Enough

Lord...You have given me anything I am or have;
I give it all back to You to stand under Your will alone.
Your love and Your grace are enough for me;
I shall ask for nothing more.

IGNATIUS OF LOYOLA

My grace is sufficient for you,
for My strength is made
perfect in weakness.

2 CORINTHIANS 12:9 NKJV

Let your faith in Christ...be in the quiet confidence
that He will every day and every moment keep
you as the apple of His eye, keep you in perfect peace
and in the sure experience of all the light and
the strength you need in His service.

ANDREW MURRAY

The Creator thinks enough of you to have sent
Someone very special so that you might have life—
abundantly, joyfully, completely, and victoriously.

I have come that they may have life,
and that they may have it more abundantly.

JOHN 10:10 NKJV

Some days, it is enough encouragement just to
watch the clouds break up and disappear,
leaving behind a blue patch of sky and bright
sunshine that is so warm upon my face.
It's a glimpse of divinity; a kiss from heaven.

Let the beloved of the LORD
rest secure in him, for
he shields him all day long.

DEUTERONOMY 33:12 NIV

God Is Patient

God is waiting for us to come to Him with
our needs.... God's throne room is always open....
Every single believer in the whole world
could walk into the throne room all at one time,
and it would not even be crowded.

CHARLES STANLEY

Lift up your eyes. Your heavenly Father waits
to bless you—in inconceivable ways to make
your life what you never dreamed it could be.

ANNE ORTLUND

God has put into each of our lives a void that
cannot be filled by the world. We may leave God
or put Him on hold, but He is always there,
patiently waiting for us...to turn back to Him.

EMILIE BARNES

To the Lord one day is as a thousand years,
and a thousand years is as one day. The Lord is
not slow in doing what he promised—the way
some people understand slowness. But God
is being patient with you. He does not want
anyone to be lost, but he wants all people
to change their hearts and lives.

2 Peter 3:8–9 ncv

God waits for us in the inner sanctuary of the soul.
He welcomes us there.

Richard J. Foster

*God is kind and merciful...
this most patient God,
extravagant in love.*

Joel 2:13 msg

Unshakable Promises

Commit to hope. There's reason to! For the believer,
hope is divinely assured things that aren't here yet!
Our hope is grounded in unshakable promises.

JACK HAYFORD

God promises to keep us in the palm of [His] hand,
with or without our awareness. God has already
made a space for us, even if we have not
made a space for God.

DAVID AND BARBARA SORENSEN

Remember you are very special to God as
His precious child. He has promised to
complete the good work He has begun in you.
As you continue to grow in Him,
He will teach you to be a blessing to others.

GARY SMALLEY AND JOHN TRENT

Faith allows us to continually delight in life
since we have placed our needs in God's hands.

JANET L. WEAVER SMITH

Confidence is not based on wishful thinking,
but in knowing that God is in control.

There are no hidden reserves in
the promises of God that are meant to
deprive them of their complete fulfillment.

HANNAH WHITALL SMITH

*Let us hold tightly without wavering
to the hope we affirm, for God can be
trusted to keep his promise.*

HEBREWS 10:23 NLT

My Father's World

When I look at the galaxies on a clear night—
when I look at the incredible brilliance of creation,
and think that this is what God is like, then
instead of feeling intimidated and diminished by it,
I am enlarged—I rejoice that I am part of it.

MADELEINE L'ENGLE

This is my Father's world;
He shines in all that's fair.
In the rustling grass I hear Him pass;
He speaks to me everywhere.

MALTBIE D. BABCOCK

Nothing can give you quite the same thrill
as the feeling that you are in harmony with the
great God of the universe who created all things.

DR. JAMES DOBSON

How beautiful it is to be alive!
To wake each morn as if the Maker's grace
Did us afresh from nothingness derive.

HENRY SEPTIMUS SUTTON

Above all give me grace to use these beauties of earth
without me and this eager stirring of life within me
as a means whereby my soul may rise from
creature to Creator, and from nature to nature's God.

JOHN BAILLIE

The earth is the LORD's, and all its fullness,
The world and those who dwell therein.

PSALM 24:1 NKJV

Promises Fulfilled

The fulfillment of God's promise depends
entirely on trusting God and his way, and then
simply embracing him and what he does.
God's promise arrives as pure gift.

ROMANS 4:16 MSG

Jesus Christ opens wide the doors of the
treasure house of God's promises,
and bids us go in and take with boldness
the riches that are ours.

CORRIE TEN BOOM

God has promised us even more than His own Son.
He's promised us power through the Spirit—
power that will help us do all that He asks of us.

JONI EARECKSON TADA

We may...depend upon God's promises,
for...He will be as good as His word.
He is so kind that He cannot deceive us,
so true that He cannot break His promise.

MATTHEW HENRY

Not one word of all the good words which the
LORD your God spoke concerning you has failed;
all have been fulfilled for you,
not one of them has failed.

JOSHUA 23:14 NASB

*Your promises have been thoroughly tested;
that is why I love them so much.*

PSALM 119:140 NLT

The Source

He is the Source. Of everything. Strength for your day.
Wisdom for your task. Comfort for your soul.
Grace for your battle. Provision for each need.
Understanding for each failure.
Assistance for every encounter.

JACK HAYFORD

We are forgiven and righteous because of
Christ's sacrifice; therefore we are pleasing to God
in spite of our failures. Christ alone is the source
of our forgiveness, freedom, joy, and purpose.

ROBERT S. MCGEE

The very life of God, epitomized in the love of God,
originates only and always with Him.

W. PHILIP KELLER

We must drink deeply from the very Source
the deep calm and peace of interior quietude and
refreshment of God, allowing the pure water
of divine grace to flow plentifully and
unceasingly from the Source itself.

MOTHER TERESA

You are never alone. In your heart of hearts,
in the place where no two people are ever alike,
Christ is waiting for you. And what you never
dared hope for springs to life.

BROTHER ROGER OF TAIZÉ

*For he satisfies the thirsty and
fills the hungry with good things.*

PSALM 107:9 NLT

Yes, when this flesh and heart shall fail,
And mortal life shall cease;
I shall profess, within the vail,
A life of joy and peace.

I Shall Profess

My love of You, O Lord, is not some vague feeling:
it is positive and certain. Your word struck into
my heart and from that moment I loved You.
Besides this, all about me, heaven and earth and all
that they contain proclaim that I should love You.

AUGUSTINE

God's children who joyously know and
claim who they are and whose they are,
will be most likely to manifest the
family likeness, just because they know
they are His children.

ALICE CHAPIN

We are His only witnesses. God is counting
on each of us. No angel has been given the job.
We are the lanterns—Christ is the light inside.

OLETA SPRAY

It is through the living witness of others
that we are drawn to God at all. It is because of
His creatures, and His work in them,
that we come to praise Him.

TERESA OF AVILA

I cannot witness that I have entered fully into
this life of perpetual communion with the Father,
but I have caught enough glimpses that I know it
to be the best, the finest, the fullest way of living.

RICHARD J. FOSTER

Sing to the LORD, praise his name;
proclaim his salvation day after day.

PSALM 96:2 NIV

Eternal Love

The LORD is like a father to his children,
tender and compassionate to those who fear him.
For he knows how weak we are;
he remembers we are only dust.
Our days on earth are like grass;
like wildflowers, we bloom and die.
The wind blows, and we are gone—
as though we had never been here.
But the love of the LORD remains forever....
The LORD has made the heavens his throne;
from there he rules over everything.

PSALM 103:13–17, 19 NLT

Amid the ebb and flow of the passing
world, our God remains unmoved,
and His throne endures forever.

ROBERT COLEMAN

The reason we can dare to risk loving others is
that "God has for Christ's sake loved us."
Think of it! We are loved eternally, totally,
individually, unreservedly! Nothing
can take God's love away.

GLORIA GAITHER

The impetus of God's love comes from within
Himself, to share with us His life and love.
It is a beautiful, eternal gift, held out to us in the
hands of love. All we have to do is say "Yes!"

JOHN POWELL

*He loves us with unfailing love;
the LORD's faithfulness endures forever.*

PSALM 117:2 NLT

Joy and Peace

God came to us because God wanted to
join us on the road, to listen to our story,
and to help us realize that we are not
walking in circles but moving toward the
house of peace and joy. This is the great
mystery...that continues to give us comfort and
consolation: we are not alone on our journey.
The God of love who gave us life sent us
[His] only Son to be with us at all times
and in all places, so that we never have to
feel lost in our struggles but always
can trust that God walks with us.

HENRI J. M. NOUWEN

Joy is the echo of God's life within us.

JOSEPH MARMION

Love comes while we rest against our
Father's chest. Joy comes when we catch
the rhythms of His heart. Peace comes when
we live in harmony with those rhythms.

KEN GIRE

Joy is not happiness so much as gladness;
it is the ecstasy of eternity in a soul
that has made peace with God
and is ready to do His will.

*May the God of hope fill you with all
joy and peace as you trust in him.*

ROMANS 15:13 NIV

Comfort Sweet

All God's glory and beauty come from within,
and there He delights to dwell. His visits
there are frequent, His conversation sweet,
His comforts refreshing, His peace
passing all understanding.

THOMAS À KEMPIS

God comforts. He doesn't pity. He picks
us up, dries our tears, soothes our fears,
and lifts our thoughts beyond the hurt.

ROBERT SCHULLER

God comforts. He lays His right hand on
the wounded soul...and He says, as if that one
were the only soul in all the universe:
O greatly beloved, fear not: peace be unto thee.

AMY CARMICHAEL

There is a place of comfort sweet
Near to the heart of God,
A place where we our Savior meet,
Near to the heart of God....
Hold us who wait before Thee
Near to the heart of God.

CLELAND B. MCAFEE

Every now and again take a good look at
something not made with hands—a mountain,
a star, the turn of a stream. There will come to you
wisdom and patience and solace and, above all,
the assurance that you are not alone in the world.

SIDNEY LOVETT

*God is our merciful Father
and the source of all comfort.*

2 CORINTHIANS 1:3 NLT

Drawn by Grace

Grace tells us that we are accepted just as we are.
We may not be the kind of people we want to be...
we may have more failures than achievements...
we may not even be happy, but we are nonetheless
accepted by God, held in His hands.

McCullough

We throw open our doors to God and discover
at the same moment that he has already thrown open
his door to us. We find ourselves standing where
we always hoped we might stand—out in the
wide open spaces of God's grace and glory.

Romans 5:2 msg

There is nothing but God's grace. We walk upon it;
we breathe it; we live and die by it; it makes the
nails and axles of the universe.

ROBERT LOUIS STEVENSON

The purpose of grace is primarily to restore our
relationship with God.... The work of grace
aims at...an ever deeper knowledge of God and
an ever closer fellowship with Him. Grace is
God drawing us to Himself.

J. I. PACKER

*He chose us in Him...to the praise
of the glory of His grace, by which
He made us accepted in the Beloved.*

EPHESIANS 1:4, 6 NKJV

Enfolded in Peace

I will let God's peace infuse every part of today.
As the chaos swirls and life's demands pull at me
on all sides, I will breathe in God's peace that
surpasses all understanding. He has promised that He
would set within me a peace too deeply planted
to be affected by unexpected or exhausting demands.

WENDY MOORE

Calm me, O Lord, as You stilled the storm,
Still me, O Lord, keep me from harm.
Let all the tumult within me cease,
Enfold me, Lord, in Your peace.

CELTIC TRADITIONAL

Nothing in all creation
is so like God as stillness.

MEISTER ECKHART

Don't fret or worry. Instead of worrying, pray.
Let petitions and praises shape your worries
into prayers, letting God know your concerns.
Before you know it, a sense of God's wholeness,
everything coming together for good,
will come and settle you down.
It's wonderful what happens when Christ
displaces worry at the center of your life.

PHILIPPIANS 4:6–7 MSG

God cannot give us a happiness and peace
apart from Himself, because it is not there.
There is no such thing.

C. S. LEWIS

*I am leaving you with a gift—
peace of mind and heart.*

JOHN 14:27 NLT

Radiant Grace

What do I love when I love You?
Not material beauty
or beauty of a temporal order;
not the brilliance of earthly light,
so welcome to our eyes;
not the sweet melody of harmony and song....
And yet, when I love Him,
it is true that I love a light
of a certain kind that I love in my inner self,
when my soul is bathed in light
that is not bound by space;
when it listens to sound that never dies away;
when it breathes fragrance that
is not borne away on the wind....
This is what I love when I love my God.

AUGUSTINE

He made you so you could share in His creation,
could love and laugh and know Him.

TED GRIFFEN

Grace creates liberated laughter.
The grace of God...is beautiful,
and it radiates joy.

KARL BARTH

Why did God give us imaginations?
Because they help unfold His kingdom.
Imagination unveils the Great Imaginer.
In the beginning, God created.
He imagined the world into being.
Every flower, animal, mountain, and rainbow
is a product of God's creative imagination.

JILL M. RICHARDSON

*For the LORD God is our
sun and our shield.
He gives us grace and glory.*

PSALM 84:11 NLT

God So Loved

Who shall separate us from the love of Christ?
Shall trouble or hardship or persecution
or famine or nakedness or danger or sword?...
No, in all these things we are more than
conquerors through him who loved us.
For I am convinced that neither death nor life,
neither angels nor demons, neither the present
nor the future, nor any powers, neither height
nor depth, nor anything else in all creation,
will be able to separate us from the love of God
that is in Christ Jesus our Lord.

ROMANS 8:35, 37–39 NIV

All the things in this world are gifts and signs
of God's love to us. The whole world
is a love letter from God.

PETER KREEFT

The grace of God means something like:
Here is your life. You might never have been,
but you are because the party wouldn't
have been complete without you.
Here is the world. Beautiful and terrible things
will happen. Don't be afraid. I am with you.
Nothing can ever separate us. It's for you
I created the universe. I love you.

FREDERICK BUECHNER

Nothing can separate you from His love,
absolutely nothing.... God is enough for time,
and God is enough for eternity. God is enough!

HANNAH WHITALL SMITH

*For God so loved the world that
he gave his one and only Son.*

JOHN 3:16 NIV

The earth shall soon dissolve like snow,
The sun forbear to shine;
But God, who called me here below,
Will be for ever mine.

Forever Grace

Grace is the dynamic outpouring of God's loving
nature that flows into and through creation
in an endless self-offering of healing, love,
illumination, and reconciliation.
It is a gift that we are free to ignore,
reject, ask for, or simply accept.

GERALD G. MAY

Grow in the grace and knowledge of our
Lord and Savior Jesus Christ. To him
be glory both now and forever! Amen.

2 PETER 3:18 NIV

This GOD of Grace, this God of Love....
All that he makes and does is honest and true:
He paid the ransom for his people,
He ordered his Covenant kept forever.

PSALM 111:4, 7–9 MSG

We have been given the breath of life, designed
with a unique, one-of-a-kind soul that exists forever—
whether we live it as a burden or a joy or with
indifference doesn't change the fact that we've
been given the gift of *being* now and forever.

WENDY MOORE

Let Jesus be in your heart, eternity in your spirit, the
world under your feet, the will of God in your actions.
And let the love of God shine forth from you.

CATHERINE OF GENOA

*Grace...invites us into life—a life that
goes on and on and on, world without end.*

ROMANS 5:21 MSG

God With Us

God gets down on His knees among us;
gets on our level and shares Himself with us.
He does not reside afar off and send
diplomatic messages, He kneels among us....
God shares Himself generously and graciously.

EUGENE PETERSON

God is not really "out there" at all.
That restless heart, questioning who you are
and why you were created, that quiet voice
that keeps calling your name is not just
out there, but dwells in you.

DAVID AND BARBARA SORENSEN

When all is said and done, the last word
is Immanuel—God-With-Us.

ISAIAH 8:10 MSG

God loves to look at us, and loves it when we
will look back at Him. Even when we try to
run away from our troubles...God will find us,
bless us, even when we feel most alone, unsure....
God will find a way to let us know that He is
with us *in this place*, wherever we are.

KATHLEEN NORRIS

You are in the Beloved...therefore infinitely dear
to the Father, unspeakably precious to Him.
You are never, not for one second, alone.

NORMAN DOWTY

My Presence will go with you,
and I will give you rest.

EXODUS 33:14 NIV

Seeking Hearts

In extravagance of soul we seek His face.
In generosity of heart, we glean His gentle touch.
In excessiveness of spirit, we love Him
and His love comes back to us a hundredfold.

TRICIA McCARY RHODES

I have been away and come back again
many times to this place. Each time I approach,
I regret ever having left. There is a peace here,
a serenity, even before I enter.
Just the idea of returning becomes a balm
for the wounds I've collected elsewhere.
Before I can finish even one knock,
the door opens wide and I am in His presence.

BARBARA FARMER

God's holy beauty comes near you,
like a spiritual scent, and it stirs your
drowsing soul.... He creates in you the
desire to find Him and run after Him—
to follow wherever He leads you,
and to press peacefully against
His heart wherever He is.

JOHN OF THE CROSS

Once the seeking heart finds God in
personal experience there will be no problem
about loving Him. To know Him is to love Him
and to know Him better is to love Him more.

A. W. TOZER

You will seek me and find me
when you seek me with all your heart.

JEREMIAH 29:13 NIV

Immeasurable Love

We are so preciously loved by God that
we cannot even comprehend it. No created being
can ever know how much and how sweetly
and tenderly God loves them. It is only
with the help of His grace that we are able to
persevere in spiritual contemplation with endless
wonder at His high, surpassing, immeasurable love
which our Lord in His goodness has for us.

JULIAN OF NORWICH

God loved us, and through his grace
he gave us a good hope and encouragement
that continues forever.

2 THESSALONIANS 2:17 NCV

The loving God we serve has immeasurable
compassion and tenderness toward
each of us throughout our lives.

DR. JAMES DOBSON

The soul is a temple, and God is silently
building it by night and by day. Precious thoughts
are building it; unselfish love is building it;
all-penetrating faith is building it.

HENRY WARD BEECHER

Our greatness rests solely on the fact that
God in His incomprehensible goodness
has bestowed His love upon us.
God does not love us because we are
so valuable; we are valuable
because God loves us.

HELMUT THIELICKE

*In this is love, not that we loved God,
but that He loved us.*

1 JOHN 4:10 NASB

New Every Morning

With God, life is eternal—both in quality and length.
There is no joy comparable to the joy of
discovering something new from God, about God.
If the continuing life is a life of joy,
we will go on discovering, learning.

EUGENIA PRICE

In the morning let our hearts gaze upon God's
love...and in the beauty of that vision, let us
go forth to meet the day.

ROY LESSIN

Take on an entirely new way of life—
a God-fashioned life, a life renewed from the
inside and working itself into your conduct as God
accurately reproduces his character in you.

EPHESIANS 4:22–24 MSG

A quiet morning with a loving God puts the events
of the upcoming day into proper perspective.

JANETTE OKE

Each dawn holds a new hope for a new plan,
making the start of each day the start of a new life.

GINA BLAIR

That is God's call to us—simply to be people who
are content to live close to Him and to renew the kind
of life in which the closeness is felt and experienced.

THOMAS MERTON

*Satisfy us in the morning with your
unfailing love, that we may sing for joy
and be glad all our days.*

PSALM 90:14 NIV

His Loving Touch

The simple fact of being...in the presence
of the Lord and of showing Him all that
I think, feel, sense, and experience,
without trying to hide anything,
must please Him. Somehow,
somewhere, I know that He loves me,
even though I do not feel that love
as I can feel a human embrace,
even though I do not hear a voice
as I hear human words of consolation....
God is greater than my senses,
greater than my thoughts,
greater than my heart.
I do believe that He touches me
in places that are unknown
even to myself.

HENRI J. M. NOUWEN

God's fingers can touch nothing
but to mold it into loveliness.

GEORGE MACDONALD

God is here! I hear His voice
While thrushes make the woods rejoice.
I touch His robe each time I place
My hand against a pansy's face.
I breathe His breath if I but pass
Verbenas trailing through the grass.
God is here! From every tree
His leafy fingers beckon me.

MADELEINE AARON

It is not objective proof of God's existence that
we want but the experience of God's presence.
That is the miracle we are really after, and
that is also, I think, the miracle that we really get.

FREDERICK BUECHNER

*God's Spirit touches our spirits
and confirms who we really are....
Father and children.*

ROMANS 8:16 MSG

Seek the Lord

If you are seeking after God, you may be sure of this:
God is seeking you much more. He is the Lover, and
you are His beloved. He has promised Himself to you.

JOHN OF THE CROSS

Ask and it will be given to you;
seek and you will find; knock and
the door will be opened to you.
For everyone who asks receives;
he who seeks finds; and to him who
knocks, the door will be opened.

MATTHEW 7:7–8 NIV

Prayer enlarges the heart until it is capable of
containing God's gift of Himself. Ask and seek,
and your heart will grow big enough
to receive Him and keep Him as your own.

MOTHER TERESA

Seek the LORD your God, and you will
find Him if you seek Him with all your
heart and with all your soul.

DEUTERONOMY 4:29 NKJV

God is not an elusive dream or a phantom to chase,
but a divine person to know. He does not avoid us,
but seeks us. When we seek Him, the
contact is instantaneous.

NEVA COYLE

To seek God means first of all
to let yourself be found by Him.

*I love those who love me; and those who
diligently seek me will find me.*

PROVERBS 8:17 NASB

Forever Mine

We are always in the presence of God....
There is never a non-sacred moment!
His presence never diminishes.
Our awareness of His presence may falter,
but the reality of His presence never changes.

MAX LUCADO

The King of love my Shepherd is,
Whose goodness faileth never;
I nothing lack if I am His,
And He is mine forever.

SIR HENRY WILLIAMS BAKER

Whom have I in heaven but you?
And earth has nothing I desire besides you.
My flesh and my heart may fail,
but God is the strength of my heart
and my portion forever.

PSALM 73:25–26 NIV

God is always on duty in the temple of your heart,
His home.... It is the place where Someone
takes your trouble and changes it into His treasure.

BARBARA JOHNSON

God is the sunshine that warms us, the rain
that melts the frost and waters the young plants.
The presence of God is a climate of strong
and bracing love, always there.

JOAN ARNOLD

We have been in God's thought
from all eternity, and in His creative love,
His attention never leaves us.

MICHAEL QUOIST

Surely goodness and mercy shall follow me
All the days of my life;
And I will dwell in the house of the LORD
Forever.

PSALM 23:6 NKJV

When we've been there ten thousand years,
Bright shining as the sun,
We've no less days to sing God's praise
Than when we'd first begun.

AUTHOR UNKNOWN[†]

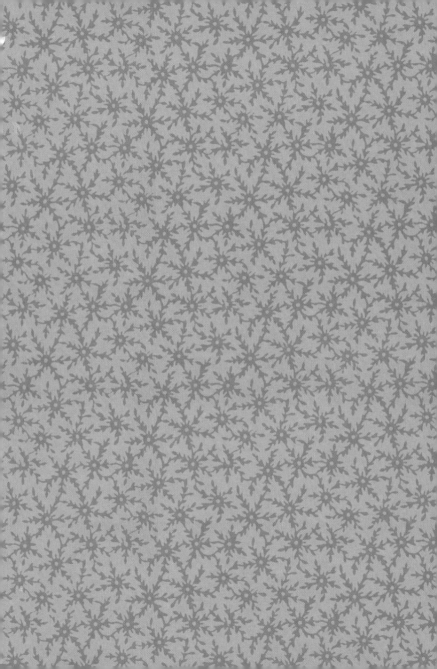

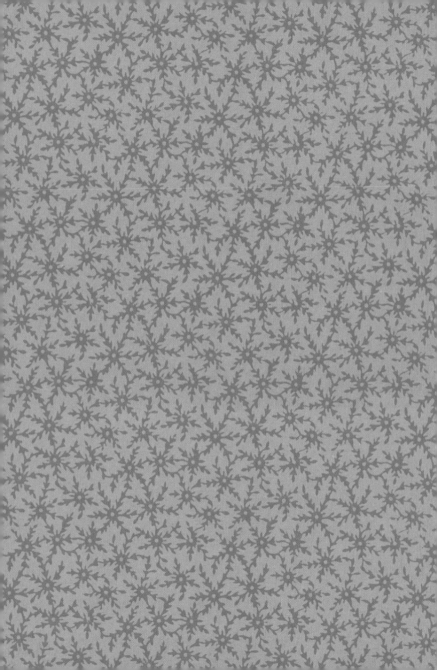